VEGETARIAN
SUSHI
MADE EASY

New York • **WEATHERHILL** • Tokyo

VEGETARIAN
SUSHI
MADE EASY

HIROKO FUKUHARA

YASUKO TAKAHATA

The recipes on pages 38–55 and page 76 were originally published in two volumes of the series *Kenko Shizenshoku Ryori* (Healthy and Natural Cuisine), *Shushoku* • *Kokumotsu* (Main Dishes and Grains) and *Fukushoku* (Side Dishes), by Pegasus in Tokyo, Japan.

First edition, 1999
Third printing, 2000

Published by Weatherhill, Inc.
41 Monroe Turnpike, Trumbull, Connecticut 06611

Printed in China

Library of Congress Cataloging-in-Publication Data Available

CONTENTS

FINGER SUSHI

SUSHI ROLLS

TOSSED SUSHI

SUSHI BALLS

SUSHI POCKETS AND PRESSED SUSHI

INTRODUCTION

Sushi originally developed in Japan, long before the invention of the refrigerator, as a means of preserving fish. The original Chinese character for sushi meant "pickled fish" or "preserved fish." In fact, the first mentions of this type of sushi, called narezushi (aged sushi), date back to the Nara period, about twelve hundred years ago. To prepare narezushi, fresh fish and salt were mixed with rice. After a period of from one month to one year, the rice naturally fermented, producing lactic acid, which cured and preserved the fish. When the fish was completely "pickled," it was removed and eaten, and the rice discarded, or used to pickle more fish or vegetables. This type of sushi is still made in all regions of Japan,

Later, in the 1500s, a faster method of preparing narezushi was invented called "namanare," or "fresh aged fish." It was "fresher" because it was only pickled for three or four days. For the first time, the rice was not discarded but eaten with the fish. Rice gradually became an important part of sushi, and the next century saw the invention of "izushi" (rice sushi), a mixture of cooked rice, rice malt, and fish and vegetables. This was followed by "quick sushi" (hayazushi) and "one-night sushi" (ichiyazushi), which were even speedier versions of the old narezushi.

Vinegar, which gives the sushi rice we know today its fresh and distinctive flavor, was first used in oshizushi, or pressed sushi, which was invented next. The rice was no longer fermented. Vinegar and seasonings were mixed in to give the desired flavor and the mixture was pressed overnight under a heavy weight. It was soon after the invention of oshizushi that sushi shops began to open up in the nation's capital, Edo—as Tokyo was called until about 1868. Oshizushi is still popular today.

From the 1700s, most of the forms of sushi still around now were invented one after another. The last type of sushi to appear is the one we all know so well today: nigirizushi, or "finger sushi," which is said to have been invented in the first decades of the nineteenth century by one Yohei, of the sushi shop Hanaya in the Ryogoku area of Edo. He came up with it as a way to prepare pressed sushi even more quickly, in the process creating what might be the very first fast food. Vinegar and seasoning were mixed into freshly cooked rice, which was then formed into a "finger" and pressed together with fresh fish or seafood. Ryogoku is on Edo Bay, from which the freshest fish was readily available. The new finger sushi spread like wildfire across Edo and has remained popular to this day, spreading out from Japan to become enjoyed around the world.

From the earliest narezushi, vegetables have been an important component of sushi, and many traditional varieties of sushi are mostly or completely vegetarian. In this book, we have assembled more than forty recipes for delicious sushi without fish. Many are traditional or based on traditional varieties of sushi eaten in Japan. Others are more innovative, but the home cook can prepare them all with confidence and assured success. We have also placed great emphasis on attractive presentation, making these recipes perfect for picnics, parties, and home dinners. But we are even more concerned with healthy eating, and sushi in all its varieties is a relatively healthy food. No oil or other fat is used in preparing it, and the acids and other organic compounds in naturally distilled vinegar aid in digestion and promoting a healthy metabolism. But most important of all is rice.

THE IMPORTANCE OF RICE

Rice is the staple food of Japanese and indeed all of Asia. Rice has several important advantages over other staple grains, such as wheat and corn. First, it is a more productive crop. A single acre planted in rice produces more than twice the grain as an acre of wheat, corn, or barley. Second, rice can be stored for long periods without losing its flavor or nutritional value, and it is easy to transport.

Third, it is simple to prepare. Wheat has a tough layer of bran, and it must be ground first and then cooked as bread or noodles before it can be eaten. The same is true of corn, for the most part. Rice, on the other hand, only needs the loosely attached chaff removed before it can be cooked whole in a pot with water. Nutritionally speaking, whole grains are also preferable to milled grains, since vitamins, oils, and other nutritional elements are inevitably lost in the milling process.

Fourth, rice is nutritionally superior to other grains. It is rich in protein, with a higher level of the crucial amino acid lysine than wheat or corn. Though wheat contains more protein than rice, the protein is inferior in quality. In fact, an exclusive rice diet can supply all the protein a healthy human needs. This is not true of a wheat diet, which is one reason that people living in wheat cultures, such as Europe, turned to animal proteins to supplement their diet. In Japan, in contrast, a rice diet has supplied in balanced form almost all nutrients necessary for growth and health. Vegetables, seaweeds, and small amounts of fish and shellfish provided any missing minerals and nutrients, and the Japanese devised methods of fermenting and processing soybeans into such foods as miso, soy sauce, and natto, which became excellent complementary protein sources.

It is important to remember that all of these statements about the nutritional superiority of rice apply to brown rice, rice with only the chaff removed and the bran completely intact. White rice is decidedly inferior to brown rice. Comparing just some of the nutritional elements in white and brown rice, we find that white rice has 91% of the calories of brown rice, but only 79% of the protein, 39% of the Vitamin B6, 28% of the niacin, 37% of the Vitamin B2, 23% of the Vitamin 1, 37% of the iron, 52% of the phosphorus, 60% of the calcium, and 28% of the fiber.

There is another important factor to consider. White rice is dead; brown rice is alive. If you plant it, and give it warmth and water, it will grow. The many vitamins, minerals, and nutrients in brown rice exist in a vital balance, the balance found in all living things, and that, too, makes it nutritionally superior to white rice in ways that we cannot yet begin to measure.

Though some of the recipes in this book are or can be made with brown rice—particularly the sushi salads—most use white rice. Sushi is meant to be aesthetically pleasing as well as delicious and nutritional, and the simple fact is that white rice usually provides a more attractive contrast to the colors of the vegetable toppings and ingredients. But then sushi, even vegetarian sushi, is a treat, not a staple, of the Japanese diet, and so perhaps the nutritional compromise is acceptable.

We have divided the recipes in this book into six groups or types.

Finger sushi, or nigirizushi

Our vegetarian finger sushi places vegetables and fruit on a bed of sushi rice, just like the fish-fillet sushi that is so popular around the world.

Sushi rolls, or makizushi

To make sushi rolls, nori is placed on a rolling mat and spread with sushi rice. Vegetable ingredients are arranged on the rice and the whole is rolled up and then cut into slices. Sushi with various decorative patterns can be made this way, and they are especially good for parties.

Tossed sushi, or chirashizushi

Vegetables are lightly cooked or otherwise prepared and then tossed in with sushi rice. These recipes are very easy to prepare, and lend themselves well to brown rice. They are perfect summer lunches.

Sushi balls, or temarizushi

A wide variety of attractive sushi can be made by forming balls of sushi rice and wrapping them or combining them with different vegetables. A soft damp cloth is used to form the balls.

Sushi pockets, or inarizushi

The pockets are made of bean curd, either deep fried or freeze dried, which is stuffed with sushi rice and other ingredients. These are perfect picnic treats.

Pressed sushi, or oshizushi.

Many of these recipes call for sushi rice in alternating layers of different colors.

The basics of sushi are easy; the variations are endless. The recipes we have presented here are just a few of the many ways in which sushi rice and vegetables can be combined in delicious, healthy, and attractive ways. We hope you'll enjoy our recipes, of course, but also that you'll go on to experiment with your own.

Here's to sushi!

BASIC INGREDIENTS

The vegetarian sushi recipes in this book use some basic ingredients that may be unfamiliar to Western cooks, but a surprising number of them are now available in well-stocked supermarkets and health-food stores. For others, you may have to visit an Asian grocery. Fortunately, these have sprung up in large numbers all over the United States in the last decade. It probably doesn't matter whether the Asian grocery in your area is operated by Americans of Korean, Chinese, Thai, Indian, or Japanese descent—most of the ingredients are used by more than one Asian culture.

Several of these ingredients are often prepared in a preliminary fashion before they are incorporated into recipes. For example, sheets of the sea vegetable called nori are often toasted lightly before being used to wrap sushi rolls. Different kinds of beans must be boiled in different ways, and dried foods must be reconstituted. Those basic preliminary techniques are described with the ingredients below.

Azuki beans
These red beans are frequently used in Japanese cooking. They are rich in complex carbohydrates, B vitamins, and minerals.

To prepare boiled azuki beans, soak 1 cup of beans in 3 cups of water overnight, then boil for 5 minutes. Drain the beans and return them to the pot. Add sufficient water to cover the beans and simmer for an additional 20 to 30 minutes, adding water as needed. This recipe makes 3 cups of boiled beans.

Bamboo shoots

Bamboo shoots are available canned in many groceries and all Asian food stores. All of the recipes in this book call for boiled, rather than fresh, bamboo shoots.

Black beans

Common in many different Asian cuisines, black beans are a variety of soy bean. Traditionally, black beans are regarded as having many medicinal properties. They are also rich in the B vitamins, iron, and calcium.

Boiling black beans in an iron pot, or placing an iron nail in the pot will insure that the beans have a beautiful shiny black color after cooking. To prepare boiled black beans, soak 1 cup of beans in 3 cups of water overnight, then boil for 30 minutes. This recipe makes 2 to 2^1/2 cups of boiled beans.

Burdock root (gobo)

Burdock is a long, thin, fibrous light brown root that is eaten only in Japan. It has an earthy taste that comes mainly from the skin, so it should not be scrubbed too roughly before cooking. A light going over with a vegetable brush is enough.

Butterburr (fuki)

Butterburr is a plant resembling rhubarb; it is also called bog rhubarb or coltsfoot. Only the stems are eaten. It has a crunchy texture and a mild taste—not at all like that of rhubarb. Butterburr is available in Japanese grocery stores.

Cucumber

Japanese cucumbers are much smaller than most Western varieties of cucumber. They are mild in taste and have few if any seeds, and the skin is smooth rather than prickly. They can be found in Asian grocery stores. You can substitute Western cucumbers if you select young, tender ones.

Chrysanthemum flowers

Chrysanthemum flowers are used in the recipes in this book for color. They can be found in Japanese food stores, or you can substitute another edible flower of the same color.

Daikon (Japanese radish) and daikon sprouts

Japanese radish is now widely available in the United States, and this long white root vegetable is very widely used in Japanese cuisine. It is grated to make sauces (mixed with soy sauce, for example, to dip sashimi), eaten raw, boiled, dried, and pickled. It is not nearly as hot as the red Western radish, but it still has a clear, sharp taste that complements oily or strongly odorous foods. It also aids digestion and warms the body.

Daikon sprouts are also sold in Asian groceries and health-food stores. They are quite hot, similar to a Western radish.

Deep-fried tofu (abura age)
Deep-fried tofu is prepared by slicing tofu thinly, removing the excess water, and deep-frying the slices in soy or rapeseed oil. This makes it high in fat, and when it is used in sushi recipes, the excess oil should be removed first by simmering the tofu slices in hot water, draining them, and patting them dry. Its unique form allows it to be cut into a sort of pocket that can then be stuffed with sushi rice or vegetables.

Fern fronds (zemmai)
Zemmai are the fronds of the royal fern, a common garden plant in the United States. Fern fronds are seasonally available—from spring to early summer—in fine grocery stores as well as Asian grocery stores . They have a bitter taste and must be boiled in salted water before eating.

Freeze-dried tofu (koyadofu)
Freeze-dried tofu is prepared by slicing tofu, freezing it, and then drying it. It is high in fats and oils, so it spoils easily and care must be taken to ensure that it is fresh. Freeze-dried tofu can be reconstituted by soaking it in warm water, but in many recipes it is used as it is, and its sponge-like texture absorbs and concentrates flavors.

Garlic Chives (nira)
Garlic chives are a chive with flat leaves that have a strong garlic odor and taste. They and their shoots (before they have leafed out) are available in Asian food stores. Select bunches with shorter leaves that are still tender and dark, lustrous green.

Ginger
Fresh ginger root (actually a tuber) is widely available in grocery stores. It must be peeled before use.

Kampyo
Kampyo is made from the bottle gourd, which is cut into long, thin strips and dried. It is used in sushi rolls and mixed with rice. To reconstitute it, sprinkle it with salt and rub it very gently before soaking it in water.

Konnyaku

Made from the root of a plant called variously devil's tongue or elephant foot, konnyaku is a grayish-brown jelly, very low in calories, composed of 97% water. It is eaten for its texture, which is rubbery. Since it has little flavor, it is often used in soups and stews, where it absorbs the flavor of the broth. Konnyaku is available in Japanese and Asian food stores in fresh, canned, and powdered instant forms.

Lotus root

Lotus root is actually the tuber of the lotus plant. It is crunchy, has a white skin, and can be eaten peeled or unpeeled. Lotus tuber is especially decorative when sliced, because it has a pattern of hollow areas that make each slice resemble an open flower.

Miso (fermented salty soybean paste, with or without cereals)

Miso is categorized into three types, depending upon the type of fermenting agent used. The lightly salted white miso that is called for in the recipes in this book uses rice as the fermenting agent. The so-called "country miso" (inaka miso) uses wheat, and hatcho miso, Nagoya miso, and tamari miso use soybeans as the fermenting agent. Miso is also categorized as sweet or salty depending upon the proportions of soybeans, fermenting agent, and salt used, and by its color—white miso, brown miso, or red miso. In Japan, miso is also often identified by its place of origin.

Mitsuba

This popular green is available in gourmet and other fine grocery stores, as well as Asian food stores. It resembles Italian parsley, which can be substituted if mitsuba is not available (cilantro has a similar but much stronger flavor). In the recipes in this book, the long stems of mitsuba are used to lightly tie pieces of sushi.

Mountain yam (yamaimo)

The mountain yam is the rounded hairy tuber of a vine native to Japan. A cultivated form of the plant is called Yamato imo. Mountain yams have a crunchy texture that is used to advantage in the recipes in this book. It is available in Japanese food stores and some health food stores.

Natto

Natto is made by fermenting simmered soybeans. Fermenting the beans makes their nutrients much more readily available for digestion, and also improves the digestibility of the foods it is eaten in combination with.

For many Westerners, natto is definitely an acquired taste—just as cheese is for many Asians. It is available in Asian food stores, usually in frozen packs.

Pickled cherry blossoms

These are sometimes available in Japanese food stores, and they make a wonderful garnish for sushi. They are also easy to make if you have a cherry tree of your own. Place about 1 cup of double pink cherry blossoms (they hold their shape better than single blossoms) in 1 cup of red plum vinegar in a bowl or pot with a lid that can be weighted down over the flowers. The weight should be heavy enough to keep the blossoms submerged, but not to crush them. After 1 week at room temperature, drain the liquid, sprinkle the blossoms with salt, and place them in a tightly sealed glass jar to preserve them.

Pickled plums (umeboshi)

Pickled plums are a healthy snack and a wonderful way to clean the palate after eating oily or starchy foods. They are a part of every traditional Japanese lunchbox. Be careful when eating an umeboshi for the first time: the flavor is very concentrated and extremely tart. They are available in Japanese food stores. Many of the recipes in this book call for pickled plum meat, which can be bought in jars at Japanese food stores, or you can simply remove the pit and shred or dice a whole pickled plum.

Pickled shiso leaves (ume shiso)

Shiso leaves are either red or green. Red shiso is used in making pickled plums, and it gives the plums their deep red coloring. The leaves are also delicious chopped and mixed with cooked rice or sushi rice. Pickled shiso leaves are available in Asian food stores.

Pumpkin (kabocha)

Japanese pumpkins are much smaller than those commonly seen in the United States. They are similar in size to the acorn squash, which can be substituted, but they can be found in Japanese and health food stores.

Rice

Short-grained Japanese rice is a must for sushi. In the United States, it is sometimes sold under the name "sushi rice." Japanese rice is also widely available in Japanese and Asian food stores. Brown rice used for sushi recipes must also be short-grained Japanese rice.

It is sometimes possible to find white rice that has not had the germ completely polished away. It is still white in color, but it is far more nutritious than polished white rice, and it is preferable when available. Depending upon the amount of bran polished away, it is called gobuzuki (50%), or shichibuzuki (70%). Rice with the bran polished away but the germ intact is called haigamai.

Sake and mirin
Both of these alcoholic beverages are distilled from rice. Ordinary sake, available at most liquor stores, is fine for cooking. Mirin is a sweet rice wine, somewhat similar to sherry. Sake and mirin are used in small amounts as flavorings and marinades.

Sea vegetables
Sea vegetables (also called seaweed) are widely used in Japanese cooking and a variety are available at Japanese food stores. Aonori is usually seen as fine flakes, packaged in a cellophane envelope. It is convenient for sprinkling over foods as a garnish. Nori is a dark green seaweed, the kind used to make sushi rolls. It is sold in large rectangular sheets, and it is usually toasted over an open flame before using, which improves its flavor. To toast nori, hold a sheet high enough above the flame to keep it from igniting, and briefly pass it evenly over the heat, one side at a time. If you look closely, you will see the nori change color slightly as it toasts from dark purple to green. Nori has a limited shelf life, even in a sealed container, and old nori does not turn green when toasted.

Kombu is a large kelp leaf, used in making soup stock. It, too, must be reconstituted by soaking in water for about 20 minutes. Before adding the kombu to the stock, cut fringes along its edges, increasing the surface area that will come into contact with the water.

Sesame, black & white
Sesame is a delicious and ubiquitous flavoring of Japanese cooking. Sesame-based foods, sauces, and condiments include sesame salt, sesame vinegar, sesame sauce, sesame miso, sesame tofu, chopped sesame seeds, parched sesame seeds, ground sesame seeds, sesame soy sauce, sesame dipping sauce, sesame paste, sesame sweets, and many foods deep fried in sesame oil. Rich in vitamins and minerals and attributed with a wide variety of medicinal effects, sesame is called "the won-

derful herb of long life" in the East. Black sesame seeds have a stronger effect than white.

One of the most commonly used sesame-based ingredients is sesame paste, which is available in Asian food stores and some natural food stores. You can easily make your own by roasting 1 cup of sesame seeds in a pan until they begin to release their oil, then grinding them in a mortar for 5 minutes until smooth. This recipe will make $1/2$ cup of paste.

Shiitake

Shiitake mushrooms are perhaps the most widely used mushrooms in Japanese cooking and most large supermarkets in the United States now stock them both fresh and dried.

Fresh shiitake are best eaten grilled and sprinkled with a little salt and then dipped in a vinegar-citrus sauce, or sauteed and served sprinkled with lemon juice. Their rich flavor is an excellent contribution to rice dishes and stews. Dried shiitake make wonderful soup stock, because their flavor is more concentrated. Shiitake are reconstituted by placing them in enough water to cover them and letting them soak for about 20 minutes. When reconstituting shiitake, it's important not to leave them in water too long, for they will gradually lose their flavor. It's also an excellent idea to use the water they've been soaked in as soup stock.

Shimeji

Shimeji are small brown button-headed mushrooms that grow in a cluster. They have a slippery texture and a nutty taste and are excellent in soups and stews. They are widely available in Japanese food stores.

Soy sauce

Soy sauce is produced by fermenting water, salt, and a yeast made from soybeans and wheat for about one year. There are three main kinds. Koikuchi soy sauce is fermented for a longer period and is thicker and darker in color. The light usukuchi soy sauce is fermented for a shorter time. Interestingly, usukuchi soy sauce actually has a higher salt content—19.6% as compared to 17.65% for koikuchi soy sauce. The variety known as tamari is sweeter than the others. Artificially brewed soy sauce, which uses amino acids and chemical processes to sidestep the natural brewing period, is now available, but it lacks the flavor, nutrition, and medicinal properties of the real thing. Soy sauce not only seasons with salt but complements and accentuates the taste of fats and oils in food. It is combined with other seasonings and flavorings to create many varieties of flavored and medicinal soy sauces.

In general, koikuchi soy sauce is used in cooking, light soy sauce is used (in smaller quantities) when preserving the natural colors of the ingredients is important, and tamari is used for dipping raw fish fillets (sashimi).

Soybeans
Soybeans are ubiquitous in Japanese cooking. Fresh green soybeans are eaten in their pods, boiled and salted, as a snack with beer or cold drinks in the summer. Dried soybeans, yellow in color, are simmered in a bean stew, sprinkled in powdered form over rice and rice cakes, and are the main ingredients of such basic Japanese foodstuffs as tofu, natto, miso, and soy sauce.

Spring onion
Japanese cooking uses two types of onion, the ordinary, round onion commonly used in Western cooking (tama negi, or "ball onion") and the "long onion" (naga negi), which is similar to our green onion but about three times as thick. Asian food stores often carry these long onions, but our green or spring onions can be substituted. In Japanese cooking, and in many of the recipes in this book, the onions are sliced in thin rounds and used as a garnish.

Tofu
Tofu is widely available in grocery stores all over the United States.

Vinegars
Japanese cooking uses vinegar as a flavoring in many dishes. Always try to have rice vinegar and red plum vinegar (umesu) on hand. Apple cider vinegar can also be used.

PREPARATION TECHNIQUES

WHITE SUSHI RICE
(Makes 7 cups)

3 cups short-grain white rice
3$^{1}/_{2}$ cups water
2 tablespoons sake
4 inches kombu
$^{1}/_{3}$ cup apple cider vinegar
1 tablespoon honey
1 tablespoon salt

Wash the rice and drain. Place in a rice cooker, add the water, sake, and kombu and let sit for one hour. Remove the kombu and cook the rice. After the cooking cycle is complete, allow the rice to sit for 15 minutes. In the meantime, mix together the vinegar, honey, and salt. Place the rice in a large, flat container and sprinkle the vinegar mixture over it. Use a flat wooden spatula to mix and turn the rice with a cutting motion while fanning it vigorously until it shines.

Yellow sushi rice can be made by adding 1 teaspoon of turmeric to the water before cooking.

Pink sushi rice can be made by substituting 1/4 cup red plum vinegar for the apple cider vinegar.

Green sushi rice can be made by folding 2 tablespoons of powdered seaweed into cooked white sushi rice.

BROWN SUSHI RICE
(Makes 6 cups)

---

3 cups short-grain brown rice
3 1/2 cups water
2 tablespoons sake
4 inches kombu
1/3 cup plum vinegar
3 tablespoons mirin

Wash the brown rice and drain. Place in a pressure cooker, add the water, sake, and kombu and let sit overnight. Place the lid on the pressure cooker and cook over medium heat until pressurized. Then cook for 20 minutes over low heat. Remove from heat and allow the rice to sit for 15 minutes. Meanwhile, mix together the plum vinegar and mirin. After cooker is depressurized completely, open it and remove the kombu. Place the rice in a large, flat container and sprinkle the vinegar mixture over it. Use a flat wooden spatula to mix and turn the rice with a cutting motion while fanning it vigorously until it shines.

RED GINGER PICKLES

---

1 cup peeled, thinly sliced fresh ginger
1/3 cup plum vinegar
2 tablespoons mirin

Place the ginger slices in a pot of boiling water and parboil for 1 minute. Remove and drain. Soak the ginger slices in the vinegar and mirin. In about 10 minutes, the ginger will become an attractive shade of red. It can be used immediately or stored in the refrigerator.

SOUP STOCK

This recipe is for the basic soup stock (dashi) that is used in many recipes in this book. Stock is made twice from the same ingredients. The first stock is cooked longer and has a stronger taste. It is the one used in most recipes. The second, much lighter stock is used when it is necessary to preserve the delicate taste of other ingredients.

---

3 dried shiitake
1 4-inch square of kombu
5 cups mineral water

FIRST STOCK (ICHIBAN DASHI)
Reconstitute the shiitake by soaking in water for about 20 minutes. Rinse the kombu and cut a fringe of 5 to 6 lines around all the edges of the square. Pour mineral water in a saucepan and simmer the shiitake and kombu in the saucepan for 30 minutes. Remove the shiitake and kombu and save the stock.

SECOND STOCK (NIBAN DASHI)
Pour 2^{1}/2 cups of water into the saucepan and place the shiitake and kombu which were used for the first stock in it. Boil for 4 or 5 minutes, then remove the shiitake and kombu.

PREPARING VEGETABLES

Cutting Techniques
A considerable part of the enjoyment of Japanese food comes from presentation, and presentation depends a great deal upon cutting techniques. Japanese cooks cut vegetables in ways that are intrinsically attractive, that provide visual variety, and that make the most of the taste and texture of the vegetable. Some of the most common cutting techniques are illustrated on the following pages.

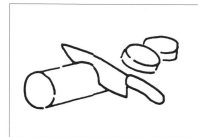

Round slices. The thickness depends upon the recipe. Used for Japanese radish, carrots, sweet potatoes, bamboo shoots, Japanese eggplants, cucumbers, lotus root, and other cylindrical vegetables. These can be trimmed with the "edging" technique described on the opposite page.

Quarter slices. These are made by cutting a long, cylindrical vegetable into four quarters and then slicing the quarters. Used for Japanese radish, turnips, carrots, potatoes, lotus roots, and other similar vegetables in stews, sauteed dishes, and soups.

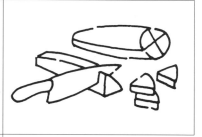

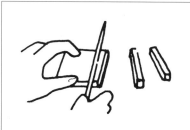

Sticks. First square a vegetable slice and then cut it into sticks, about 2 inches long and 3/8 inches square. Used for potatoes, Japanese radish, cucumbers, carrots, and similar vegetables when making pickles or stews.

Rough cut. Make alternate slices at opposing angles, resulting in pieces of different shapes but of roughly the same size. Used for long, cylindrical vegetables such as cucumbers, Japanese eggplants, burdock, carrots, and potatoes, mostly in stews.

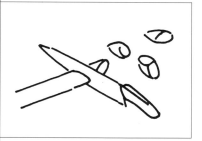

Wedges. First cut a round vegetable in half, and then divide that half into two to four wedges. Used for onions, pumpkin, and squash in stews and sauteed dishes, and for other fruits and vegetables in salads and desserts.

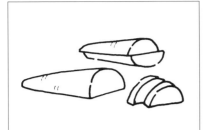

Half-moon slices. Cut round slices in half. Used for Japanese radish, carrots, lotus root, sweet potatoes, bamboo shoots, and tomatoes in stews, fried dishes, soups, and as pickles.

Matchsticks. Square the vegetable and cut into matchsticks about ¹/₄ inches on a side. Used for Japanese radish, burdock, carrots, and cucumbers in salads, simmered vegetable dishes, and soups.

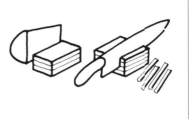

Slivers. Cut even thinner than matchsticks. Cut in the direction of the vegetable fibers to keep the vegetable from disintegrating. For Japanese radishes, carrots, cucumbers, ginger root, and onions in salads and soups.

Edging. Trim the edges of large pieces of vegetable for a beveling effect when cooking them in stews. This will preserve their shape and is very attractive. Used for Japanese radish, turnips, carrots, and potatoes.

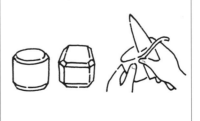

Chopping. Cut thin slices of bunches of round vegetables for garnishes or sauteed dishes. Used for spring onions, garlic chives, and cucumbers.

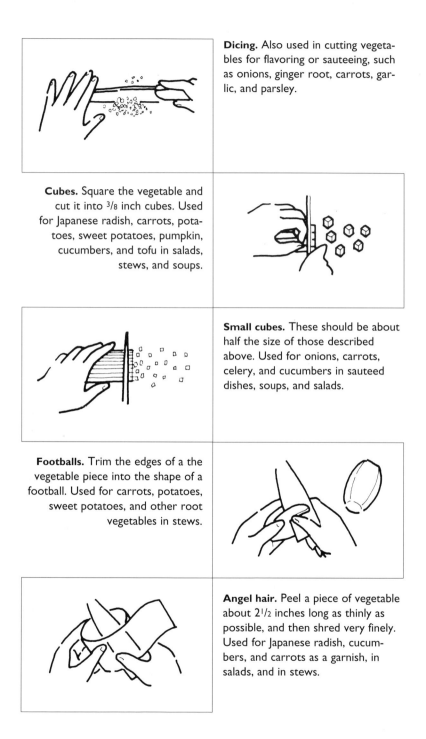

Dicing. Also used in cutting vegetables for flavoring or sauteeing, such as onions, ginger root, carrots, garlic, and parsley.

Cubes. Square the vegetable and cut it into 3/8 inch cubes. Used for Japanese radish, carrots, potatoes, sweet potatoes, pumpkin, cucumbers, and tofu in salads, stews, and soups.

Small cubes. These should be about half the size of those described above. Used for onions, carrots, celery, and cucumbers in sauteed dishes, soups, and salads.

Footballs. Trim the edges of a the vegetable piece into the shape of a football. Used for carrots, potatoes, sweet potatoes, and other root vegetables in stews.

Angel hair. Peel a piece of vegetable about 2 1/2 inches long as thinly as possible, and then shred very finely. Used for Japanese radish, cucumbers, and carrots as a garnish, in salads, and in stews.

Cooking Techniques

Two basic cooking techniques are used in preparing the vegetables for vegetarian sushi: parboiling and longer simmering. Unlike in some Western vegetarian cuisines, the vegetables in vegetarian sushi are almost never eaten raw (even cucumbers and onions are salted or soaked before use), except when they are a garnish.

• When the goal is to bring out the natural flavor, freshness, and texture of the vegetable, it is parboiled. This method is used to prepare such vegetables as asparagus, broccoli, carrots, green beans, green peas, Japanese pumpkin, lotus root, shimeji, snow peas, and spinach. Specific instructions are provided in the recipes, but in general take care not to overcook the vegetables.

• When the goal is to impart or concentrate a flavor, the vegetable is simmered in stock, soy sauce, and mirin for a longer time. This method is used to prepare such vegetables and ingredients as bamboo shoots, butterburr, kampyo, konnyaku, and deep-fried and freeze-dried tofu.

SUSHI-MAKING TECHNIQUES

Forming sushi rice into fingers, rolls, balls, and stuffed pockets is actually very easy once you get the hang of it, but it may require a little experimentation for one unused to working with Japanese rice, which is sticky rather than dry and flaky. When handling sushi rice, make certain your hands are very clean. To keep the rice from sticking to your hands, and for hygienic purposes, also wet your hands lightly with clean water into which you've mixed some vinegar.

Finger Sushi

Form finger sushi by scooping up a small amount of rice with your forefinger and second finger of your right hand and placing it in your cupped left palm. Use the fingers and thumb of your right hand to form it onto a long, narrow mound in your cupped palm. Press enough to make the rice hold firmly together, but not too hard, or it will stick to your hand. You can then lift the finger of rice out of your palm and place the vegetable topping on it. You may need to press the topping down lightly with your fingers and adjust the shape of the rice accordingly to form an attractive piece of finger sushi.

Sushi Rolls

You need a rolling mat to form sushi rolls. These small bamboo mats are available in Japanese and Asian food stores. Set the mat down so that it rolls up away from you. Most sushi rolls are made by first placing a sheet of toasted nori on the mat. Some recipes ask you to join two sheets of nori together. Crush a few grains of sushi rice between the overlapping seams. This acts as a paste that holds the sheets together firmly.

Next, wet your hands with water and vinegar and place the appropriate amount of rice on the mat, spreading it out to the required thickness in an even layer. Each recipe contains specific instructions for arranging the ingredients on the bed of rice. Some suggest that you turn the mat 90 degrees to make manipulation of the fillings easier. But in the end, you usually roll up the mat by lifting the edge closest to you and rolling away from yourself. When the bamboo mat is completely rolled up, lightly squeeze it to firm up the roll and make it stick together.

Allow the roll to set for a few minutes, then cut it with a sharp knife, wiping the knife against a clean cloth after every cut.

Sushi Balls

Wet your hands with water and vinegar and form small sushi balls by pressing the rice with the thumb and fingers of one hand against the cupped palm of the other.

Sushi Pockets

Sushi pockets are prepared from sheets of deep-fried tofu. Instructions are given in the specific recipes. To stuff a pocket, wet your hands with water and vinegar, scoop up a small amount of rice, and press it into the pocket.

FINGER
SUSHI

VEGETABLE-WRAPPED FINGER SUSHI

(Makes 9 pieces, 3 of each variety)

In this sushi, thin vegetable slices are wrapped completely around the rice.

---

2 cups white sushi rice

3 thin slices Japanese radish (daikon)
3 thin slices carrot
3 thin slices Japanese cucumber

GARNISHES
daikon sprouts and sliced radish
thinly sliced okra
red onion cubes
red ginger pickles

Slice the Japanese radish, carrot, and cucumber vertically, making thin slices about 3 inches long, to be wrapped around the sushi rice as in the photograph. Parboil the daikon and carrot slices in lightly salted water, rinse, and soak in salted water. Soak the cucumber slices in lightly salted water.

Shape small amounts of sushi rice into fingers and wrap each with one of the three vegetable slices.

Garnish the daikon sushi with daikon sprouts and radish slices, the carrot with okra slices, and the cucumber with cubes of red onion. Serve with red ginger pickles.

LOTUS-ROOT SUSHI
(Makes 12 pieces)

Lotus tuber has a deliciously crunchy texture that contrasts nicely with sushi rice. Its attractive "flower" pattern when sliced makes this sushi a visual treat as well.

---

2 cups white sushi rice
1 tablespoon white sesame seeds

¹/₂ lotus root tuber
¹/₄ medium carrot
8 mitsuba stems
red ginger pickles and shredded pickled plum as a garnish

Lightly toast the sesame seeds in a nonstick pan without oil, then place in a mortar and crush roughly (do not grind to a paste). Mix with the sushi rice.

Slice the lotus root into thin round slices and simmer in 2 cups water and 1 teaspoon vinegar for 3 minutes.

Cut the carrot into 1¹/₂ inch lengths and slice into thin sheets. Parboil in lightly salted water.

Soften the mitsuba stems slightly by dipping them quickly in boiling water.

Shape a small amount of the sushi rice into a finger shape, as for finger sushi. Place a layer of carrot on top the rice, then a lotus slice. Tie with a piece of mitsuba and garnish with a dab of shredded pickled plum. Serve with red ginger pickles.

BAMBOO-SHOOT FINGER SUSHI
(Makes 8 pieces)

Boiled bamboo shoots are widely available in cans from Oriental markets. Pickled cherry blossoms are also available, but you can make your own, too. See page 15 for a recipe.

---

2 cups brown sushi rice
3 tablespoons ground white sesame seeds

1 medium boiled bamboo shoot
2 cups soup stock
2 tablespoons light soy sauce
2 tablespoons sake

8 mitsuba stems
8 pickled cherry blossoms
red ginger pickles

To make thin slices of bamboo shoot to wrap around the sushi rice, hold the bamboo shoot in your hand and peel it as you would peel an apple into thin strips about 2 inches long. Simmer the bamboo shoot strips in the soup stock, light soy sauce, and sake for 8 minutes.

The cross-hatched grill marks on the bamboo shoots in the photograph were made with a heated metal barbecue skewer. This simulates the appearance of a fish fillet, and is an optional decorative touch.

Soften the mitsuba stems slightly by dipping them quickly in boiling water.

Form a small amount of sushi rice into a finger and wrap it with a slice of boiled bamboo. Tie with a mitsuba stem and decorate with pickled cherry blossoms. Serve with a garnish of red ginger pickles.

FRUIT CANAPE FINGER SUSHI
(Makes 4 pieces of each of the 4 varieties)

This is an innovative combination of fruit and sushi rice in an upside-down combination of rice on a slice of fruit. Loquat, called biwa in Japanese, is a small yellow fruit with a firm, smooth texture and a mild taste. Cut it in half and remove the large seeds before slicing.

---

2 cups white sushi rice
2 tablespoons white sesame seed

4 slices about 2 inches in diameter of loquat, papaya,
    mango, or apricot
small amounts of kiwi, apple, pineapple, and radish

4 slices of apple, cut in quarters about 2 inches across
small amounts of kiwi, carrot, and loquat

4 slices of pineapple, cut in quarters about 2 inches across
small amounts of grapefruit, parsley, apple, and kiwi

1 kiwi, ends trimmed off and cut into 4 equal slices
small amounts of apple and raisins

parsley and cherries as garnish

Stir the sesame seeds into the sushi rice.

Prepare the 4 varieties of fruit slices as above.

Place a finger of sushi rice on the large fruit slices and decorate with small amounts of the fruits and vegetables noted above. Serve on a platter garnished with parsley and cherries.

VEGETABLE FINGER SUSHI
(Makes 14 pieces, 2 of each variety)

This is a vegetarian interpretation of finger sushi (nigirizushi), the variety most familiar to Westerners. Here the raw fish that sits atop the rice is replaced with 7 different vegetables. You can of course come up with new variations of your own.

---

3 cups white sushi rice
nori as needed, toasted and cut into strips

TOPPINGS
2 medium asparagus spears
$^1/_3$ cup Japanese pumpkin, cut into matchsticks
$^1/_3$ cup carrot, cut into matchsticks
$^1/_4$ avocado
$^1/_3$ Japanese cucumber
2 shiitake
1 tablespoon soy sauce
1 tablespoon mirin
2 cherry tomatoes

GARNISHES
1 spring onion, sliced fine
1 inch piece of fresh peeled ginger root, cut into matchsticks
$^1/_2$ teaspoon shredded pickled plum
1 pinch poppy seed

Prepare the toppings for the seven kinds of vegetable finger sushi as follows:

1. Parboil the asparagus in lightly salted water and cut into 2-inch lengths.
2. Julienne the pumpkin and parboil in lightly salted water.
3. Slice the carrot into thin rectangles about $^3/_4$ inches by 1$^1/_2$ inches and parboil in lightly salted water. After draining the carrots, lay them out in a row, overlapping the edges slightly.
4. Cut the avocado into rectangles about $^3/_4$ inches by 1$^1/_2$ inches.

5. Slice the cucumber thinly into 1½ inch slices and lay them out in a row, overlapping the edges slightly.
6. Reconstitute the shiitake in 1 cup of water for about 1 hour, then add
1 tablespoon soy sauce and 1 tablespoon mirin to the water and simmer for about 8 minutes.
7. Slice the cherry tomatoes.

Make a sushi finger from the sushi rice and place one of the ingredients on top of the sushi as in the photograph. Wrap a band of nori around the piece. It is customary to make sushi in pairs, so make two of each variety.

No garnish is necessary for the asparagus, pumpkin, or carrot sushi. Garnish the avocado sushi with a ginger matchstick. Place a dab of shredded pickled plum on the cucumber sushi. Sprinkle the poppy seeds over the shiitake sushi. Garnish the tomato sushi with the spring onion slices.

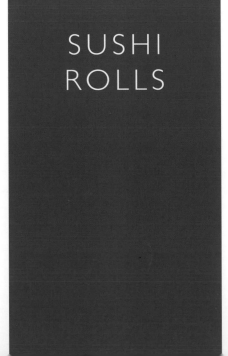

SUSHI
ROLLS

SPIRAL SUSHI ROLLS
(Makes 1 roll, cut into 8 pieces)

These spiral rolls have accents of orange (carrot), green (green beans), and yellow (chrysanthemum flowers). You can substitute nasturtium or other edible flowers if chrysanthemum flowers are not available, or Japanese pumpkin cut into matchsticks.

---

2 1/2 cups white sushi rice
2 sheets nori

1/5 medium carrot
5 green beans
1/4 yellow chrysanthemum flower
1 tablespoon red ginger pickles
4 dried shiitake, reconstituted in 1 cup water
1 tablespoon mirin
1 tablespoon sake
2 tablespoons soy sauce

Lightly toast the nori.

Parboil the carrot and slice into matchsticks.

Parboil the green beans.

Parboil the chrysanthemum.

Place the shiitake and the 1 cup water for reconstituting in a pan. Add 1 tablespoon each of mirin and sake, and 2 tablespoons of soy sauce. Simmer over medium heat until the liquid evaporates, then slice the shiitake into 1/2 inch slices.

Join two sheets of nori by dampening the adjacent edges and overlapping them about 1/2 inch. Place this double sheet on a rolling mat. Part of the nori will extend beyond the mat (fig.1).

Spread the rice evenly over the nori, leaving about 1/4 inch of nori showing on both sides.

Arrange the vegetables in vertical rows at even intervals across the bed of rice (fig. 2). Then roll the sushi up from one side, so that the outer layer of nori forms a spiral (fig. 3).

Slice into 8 pieces with a very sharp wet knife, wiping the blade clean with a damp towel after each cut.

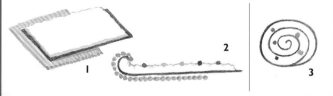

PLUM-BLOSSOMS SUSHI ROLLS
(Makes 1 roll, cut into 8 pieces)

Plum blossoms are a sign of spring in Japan. These are made with five small pink rolls—the petals—grouped around a small yellow roll for the stamens in the center.

---

1 $1/2$ **cups white sushi rice**
1 cup pink sushi rice
$1/5$ **cup yellow sushi rice**
1 sheet nori (full size)
1 $1/2$-**sheets of nori, cut into 6 $1/4$ sheets**

Lightly toast the nori. Place a $1/4$ sheet of nori on the mat, spread it evenly with $1/5$ of the pink rice, and roll. Repeat until you have five narrow rolls. Use the last $1/4$ sheet and the yellow rice to make a yellow roll.

Hold the rolling mat loosely in one hand and place the narrow rolls in its center, arranging the five pink rolls around the yellow roll to resemble five pink petals around the yellow center of a plum blossom (fig. 1). Wrap the arrangement with the mat and place a rubber band around it. Let it sit for a few minutes.

Place a sheet of nori on another rolling mat and spread most of the white rice evenly over it, reserving a small amount for later. Unroll the plum blossom from its mat and place it in the center of the white rice (fig. 2). Roll up the mat from both sides, adding the reserved white rice as necessary to round out the roll.

Slice into 8 pieces with a very sharp wet knife, wiping the blade clean with a damp towel after each cut.

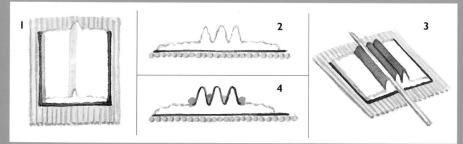

TWO-FLOWER SUSHI ROLLS
(Makes 1 roll, cut into 8 pieces)

By cleverly shaping nori-covered "hills" and "valleys" filled with colored sushi rice and green vegetables, you can create a pretty pattern of pink and yellow flowers and green leaves.

---

2 cups white sushi rice
$1/5$ cup yellow sushi rice
$1/5$ cup pink sushi rice
2 sheets nori
a small amount of boiled green vegetable, such as spinach or chopped snow peas

---

Lightly toast the nori. Place it on a rolling mat. Spread the white sushi rice over the nori, leaving about $1/4$ inch of nori free on the near and far edges.

Make a ridge of white sushi rice running vertically across the middle of the nori (fig.1), then make two more ridges, one on each side, for a total of three (fig.2).

Place the second sheet of nori lightly over these three ridges, and using a long cooking chopstick, press the nori down into the valleys between the ridges (fig. 3).

Fill one of these valleys with yellow rice and the other with pink rice. Place a line of the boiled greens along the outside of the two outermost ridges (fig.4), lift the mat, and roll from both sides.

Slice into 8 pieces with a very sharp wet knife, wiping the blade clean with a damp towel after each cut.

HEART SUSHI ROLLS
(Makes 1 roll, cut into 8 pieces)

Sushi is perfect for every occasion—even Valentine's Day.

1 cup pink sushi rice
1¹/₂ cups white sushi rice
2 sheets nori

Lightly toast the nori.

Place 1 sheet of nori on the rolling mat and spread the pink rice over it evenly. Turn the mat sideways and bring the left and right sides together to create a heart shape (fig.1). Remove the heart-shaped roll from the mat and set aside (fig. 2).

Place another sheet of nori on the rolling mat and spread most of the white rice over it evenly, reserving some for later. Make a small ridge of rice down the center of the mat, running top to bottom. Set the indentation of the heart-shaped roll (the "top" of the heart) so that it rests on this ridge (fig. 3).

Turn the mat back to its original position and roll the white rice completely around the heart, adding the reserved white rice to both sides of the heart as necessary (fig. 4).

Slice into 8 pieces with a very sharp wet knife, wiping the blade clean with a damp towel after each cut.

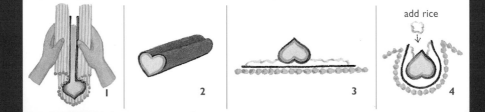

add rice

1 2 3 4

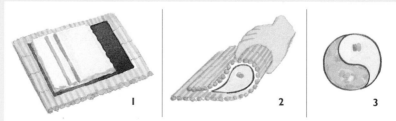

1   2   3

YIN-YANG PATTERN SUSHI ROLLS

(Makes I roll, cut into 8 pieces)

The yin-yang symbol of interlocking commas is a representation of the intimate relationship of the positive (yang) and negative (yin) energies in the cosmos. Another name for this decorative roll is tomoe, or "comma," sushi.

---

1 1/3 **cups yellow sushi rice**
1 1/3 **cups pink sushi rice**
2 sheets nori

1/4 **chrysanthemum flower**
1/3 **bunch boiled spinach**
I **tablespoon red ginger pickles, cut into somewhat thick matchsticks**

Lightly toast the nori. Parboil the chrysanthemum flower in boiling water with a dash of vinegar, then drain. (If chrysanthemum flower is not available, cut 1 1/4 inches of carrot into thin matchsticks and parboil in lightly salted water.) Place a sheet of nori on the rolling mat and then spread yellow sushi rice over about 2/3 of the nori, as shown. Place a line of red ginger pickles and spinach in the middle of the rice (fig. I). Fold the rolling mat in half and make a roll. Use your fingertips to put pressure on the end of the roll and shape it into a teardrop (half of the yin-yang symbol), as shown in figure 2. Prepare the pink rice in the same way, using lines of spinach and chrysanthemum flower or carrot. Place the yin and yang rolls together in interlocking fashion and roll together (fig. 3). Keep them in the rolling mat for a few minutes to bond them. Use a very sharp wet knife, wiped with a clean cloth after each cut, to slice the roll into 8 equal pieces.

COIN-PATTERN SUSHI ROLLS
(Makes 1 roll, cut into 8 pieces)

The design of this sushi mimics the old square coins with a hole in the center used in Japan in the days of the samurai.

---

2 cups white sushi rice
1/2 cup yellow sushi rice
1 cup pink sushi rice
3 sheets nori
1 sheet nori, cut in half

1 tablespoon red ginger pickles, cut in sticks
1/3 bunch boiled spinach

Lightly toast the nori. Place 1 of the 1/2 sheets of nori on the rolling mat. Spread 1/2 of the yellow rice in a strip about 3/4 inches wide across the nori. Place lines of spinach and red ginger pickles on this strip of rice, then spread the remaining yellow rice on top. Form it into a square shape about 1 1/2 inches on a side, as shown in fig. 1. Set aside.

Join two full pieces of nori by smashing a few sushi rice grains between their edges as a paste and place on a rolling mat. Spread pink sushi rice on 1/3 of the nori nearest you and spread white rice on the rest, leaving about 3/4 inches of nori on the far end. (fig. 2) Roll the mat up firmly from the end nearest you, creating a whirlpool pattern. Cut the roll into quarters lengthwise, as shown in fig. 2.

Join a full piece of nori to a 1/2 piece of nori and set it on the rolling mat. Place two of the 1/4 whirlpool rolls on the seaweed, the cut edges facing out. Rest the square yellow rice roll on top of them. (fig. 3) Place the two remaining 1/4 whirlpool rolls on top, their cut edges also facing out. Roll everything together, taking care to preserve square corners so that the final roll is square in shape (fig. 4).

Use a very sharp wet knife, wiped with a clean cloth after each cut, to slice the roll into 8 equal pieces.

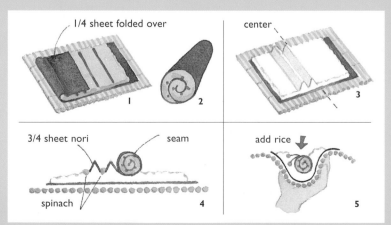

1/4 sheet folded over

1

2

center

3

3/4 sheet nori   seam

spinach   4

add rice

5

SNAIL SUSHI ROLLS
(Makes 1 roll, cut into 8 pieces)

---

2 cups white sushi rice
1 cup pink sushi rice
2 full sheets nori
1 ^{3}/4-sheet nori
1 ^{1}/4-sheet nori

a small amount of carrot cut into matchsticks
^{1}/2 bunch spinach

Lightly toast the nori. Parboil the carrot in lightly salted water. Blanch the spinach and firmly wring out all excess water.

Place a sheet of nori horizontally on the rolling mat and spread the pink rice evenly over it, leaving about ^{3}/4 inch open at the far edge.

By pressing a wet cooking chopstick or similar utensil into the rice, make 5 or 6 evenly spaced grooves and lay the chopped carrots down into them. From the close edge, fold over ^{1}/4 of the rice-covered nori (fig. 1), then roll up the mat from the near edge, making a snail-shell pattern when seen from the end (fig. 2). Set the roll aside.

Place a sheet of nori horizontally on the rolling mat and spread 2 cups of white sushi rice over the nori, reserving about ^{3}/4 inches on the far edge and ^{1}/2 inch on the near edge. Make two ridges of rice about ^{1}/2-inch high on the near side of center (fig. 3).

Cover the ridges with the ^{3}/4 sheet nori, and then twist the spinach and lay it down in two lines, one between the ridges and the other on the near side of the second ridge (fig. 4).

Place the pink sushi roll in the center of the white sushi, the nori seam face up. Turn the entire rolling mat 90 degrees and lift from below, bringing the two ends of the mat slowly together. Fill in at the top of the roll with the remaining white sushi rice to make the roll round, and roll up firmly (fig. 5).

With the seam of the nori facing down, use a very sharp wet knife, wiped with a clean cloth after each cut, to slice the roll into 8 equal pieces.

ROSE-PATTERN SUSHI ROLLS
(Makes 1 roll, cut into 8 pieces)

A rose is a rose is a rose—even when it's made of sushi! Though not a traditional Japanese pattern, here's a fine example of the kind of experimenting you can do with visual patterns in sushi rolls.

---

2 cups white sushi rice
²/₃ cup pink sushi rice
3 full sheets nori
¹/₃ sheet nori
¹/₆ sheet nori

5 to 6 parboiled strings beans
1 ¹/₂ tablespoons red ginger pickles, cut in thin strips

Lightly toast the nori. Cut off both ends of the beans.

Join two pieces of nori by wetting the adjoining short edges and place on a rolling mat. Spread the pink rice very thinly across the entire double sheet of nori, about 1 rice grain deep (fig. 1). Sprinkle the ginger over it and roll firmly from the edge nearest to you.

Place another sheet of nori the long way on the rolling mat. Reserve about 2 cups of the white rice, and spread the remainder over the nori, leaving about ³/₄ inch open on the far edge of the sheet and ¹/₂ inch open on the near edge. Use a long cooking chopstick or a similar utensil to press three grooves in the white rice, as shown in the figure—a single groove to one side of center and two grooves, about ¹/₂ inch apart, on the other side of center (fig. 2).

Place a ¹/₃ sheet of nori over the single groove and the ¹/₆ sheet strip over the two grooves (fig. 3). Press the beans lightly into the grooves, seams down. If you can't fill the entire groove with a single bean, use two, carefully cutting and matching the ends.

Place the roll of pink rice between the grooves of nori and beans and turn the mat 90 degrees. Lift it from the bottom, slowly bringing both ends together. Use the rice you reserved to fill in at the top, just under the seam, to make the roll round and the "rose" centered in it (fig. 4). Roll together firmly.

With the seam of the nori facing down, use a very sharp wet knife, wiped with a clean cloth after each cut, to slice the roll into 8 pieces.

2.5–3 inches

0.5 inch

bean   roll (see above)

1/4 sheet of nori   1/6 sheet of nori

add rice

WISTERIA-SPRAY SUSHI ROLLS
(Makes 1 roll)

By ingenious cutting and "unfolding," these teardrop-shaped sushi rolls are made to resemble the drooping flowers of the wisteria, a much-loved flower in Japan.

---

¹/₃ cup yellow sushi rice
¹/₃ cup pink sushi rice
1 sheet nori, cut in half

Lightly toast the nori. Place ¹/₂ sheet nori on the rolling mat and spread the yellow rice in the center, as shown in figure 1. Fold the nori in half and shape it into a teardrop shape.

Repeat the process with the pink sushi rice. Align the two rolls as in figure 2 and cut in the direction of the arrow with a very sharp wet knife, wiped with a damp cloth after each cut. Align the cut rolls and cut again as in figure 3, in the direction of the arrow.

Once again cut through the rolls, being careful this time not to cut the bottom layer of nori. Open out the roll along the cut, as in figure 4.

Place the 2 strings of 4 rolls end to end in a serving bowl.

AVOCADO ROLLS
(Makes 2 rolls, 8 pieces each)

Avocado rolls are a staple of sushi shops in the United States, but almost unheard of in Japan. Here's a Japanese take on a popular Western sushi innovation.

---

2 cups white sushi rice

1 1/4 inches carrot
2 sheets nori
4 leaves lettuce
1 ripe avocado
a small amount of shredded pickled plum

ADDITIONAL DECORATION
1 radish
1/4 avocado
1/3 bunch daikon sprouts
1/3 bunch shimeji mushrooms
4 slices carrot, cut in the shape of a gourd
a small amount of shredded pickled plum

Peel the avocado carefully and cut into long strips 1/3 inch on each side.

Cut the carrot into matchsticks and parboil in lightly salted water.

Place a sheet of nori on the rolling mat and spread the sushi rice over it evenly. First place the lettuce leaf, then place the avocado and carrot on top, in the center. Roll firmly. Cut at a slight angle and serve with a dab of shredded pickled plum on each slice.

Slice the radish thinly and soak in salt water for about 5 minutes, until the slices wrinkle.

Peel another avocado and cut a quarter out of it. Place the quarter on the plate and top with the daikon sprouts, shimeji, radish, and shredded pickled plum, and a gourd-shaped carrot slice.

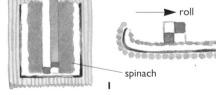

roll

spinach

1

2

CHECKERBOARD SUSHI
(Makes 1 roll, cut into 8 pieces)

This checkerboard pattern is called the Ichimatsu pattern in Japan. It was named after a Kabuki actor who made a big hit when he wore a dramatic checked costume. It has been a popular design motif for centuries, and looks just as good on sushi as it does onstage.

---

2 cups white sushi rice

1 medium carrot
¹/₂ mountain yam
1 bunch spinach or other green leafy vegetable
2 sheets nori
red ginger pickles as garnish

Cut the carrot and mountain yam into long sticks about ¹/₃ inch on a side. Parboil the carrot and the spinach (separately) in lightly salted water.

Place the nori on the rolling mat and spread the sushi rice over it evenly. Spread the spinach over most of the rice, then place the mountain yam and carrot sticks in the center in two layers: 1 carrot and 1 mountain yam on the bottom, then alternated on the top to create a checkerboard pattern when seen from the end. Roll firmly.

Cut the roll into 8 pieces and serve cut side up. Garnish with red ginger pickles.

SHINODA SUSHI ROLLS
(Makes 2 rolls, each cut into 4 pieces)

Shinoda was the name of a forest in Osaka associated with a legend about foxes, which are magical tricksters in Japanese folklore. Foxes were also believed to be very fond of deep-fried tofu, the wrapping for these sushi rolls.

---

2 rice bowls of white sushi rice

2 large deep-fried tofu pockets
1 1/2 cups soup stock
2 tablespoons mirin
1 tablespoon sake
1 tablespoon soy sauce

1 1/2 medium carrots
6 green beans
8 stems mitsuba
8 pickled cherry blossoms
red ginger pickles as garnish

Pour boiling water over the deep-fried tofu pockets, and then rinse and dry to remove excess oil. Cut three edges of the pockets and fold them out into flat sheets. Simmer in the soup stock, mirin, sake, and soy sauce for 4 to 5 minutes.

Chop 1 carrot into thin slices, then parboil in lightly salted water. Drain. Cut the 1/2 carrot into cubes and parboil in lightly salted water. Drain.

Parboil the beans in lightly salted water as well.

Place the sheet of deep-fried tofu on the rolling mat and cover the entire sheet with a layer of the parboiled carrot slices. Spread the sushi rice evenly on top the layer of carrot, and then place the carrot cubes and beans in a line down the center of the rice (fig. 1). Roll up the mat. Cut the roll into 4 equal pieces and tie each with a mitsuba stem (fig. 2). Serve with the pickled cherry blossoms and red ginger pickles as a garnish.

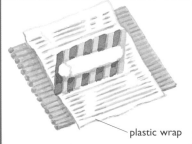

plastic wrap

BARBER POLE SUSHI
(Makes 2 rolls each of the carrot and shiitake rolls, a total of 24 pieces)

The original name for this sushi is tazuna sushi, or "horse-reins sushi." In old Japan, decorative horse reins were made of two colors of rope twisted together, creating a spiral design much like our barber poles.

---

2 cups white sushi rice

I medium carrot
I Japanese cucumber

8 dried shiitake
2 cups soup stock
2 tablespoons mirin
2 tablespoons soy sauce
2 tablespoons sake

red ginger pickles

Slice the carrot vertically into thin slices and parboil quickly in lightly salted water.

Cut the cucumber into long vertical slices and soak in lightly salted water.

Soak the shiitake in water for about twenty minutes to reconstitute them, then simmer in the soup stock, mirin, soy sauce, and sake for 8 minutes. Remove and cut into thin slices.

Place a layer of plastic wrap on the rolling mat and arrange the carrot slices and the cucumber slices in alternating rows, 5 of each vegetable. Place the sushi rice on top of the carrot and cucumber in a long roll, like a rolling pin. Firmly roll the combination up. The carrot and cucumber will be the wrap on the outside, and the rice on the inside.

Follow the same procedure to prepare shiitake rolls.

Remove the plastic wrap from the rolls, cut each into 6 equal pieces, and serve with a garnish of red ginger pickles.

SUSHI CONES
(Makes 10 rolls, 2 of each kind)

This is a perfect "do-it-yourself" sushi that party or dinner guests can make themselves if you prepare and set out the ingredients.

---

2 cups brown sushi rice
2¹/₂ sheets toasted nori

¹/₈ block konnyaku
¹/₃ cup soup stock
1 teaspoon soy sauce
¹/₂ teaspoon mirin
¹/₅ medium carrot
2 asparagus spears

¹/₂ cup natto
1 teaspoon soy sauce
¹/₂ teaspoon seaweed flakes (to sprinkle on natto)
¹/₃ Japanese cucumber

¹/₃ cup mountain yam, cut into sticks
2 stems chives
1 tablespoon shredded pickled plum

20 daikon sprouts
1 tablespoon miso
2 cherry tomatoes

¹/₃ cup shimeji mushrooms
1 teaspoon soy sauce
2 leaves lettuce, torn into bite-size pieces

Cut the sheet of toasted nori into quarters (fig. 1).
    Prepare the ingredients for the five kinds of cones as follows:

1. Cut the konnyaku into strips and simmer for about 5 minutes in ¹/₃ cup soup stock, 1 teaspoon soy sauce, and ¹/₂ teaspoon mirin. Cut the carrot into thin sticks and parboil, with the asparagus, in lightly salted water.
2. Stir the soy sauce into the natto and sprinkle the seaweed flakes over it. Cut the cucumber into sticks.

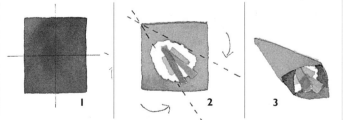

1   2   3

3. Cut the mountain yam into sticks. Chop the chives into $1/3$-inch lengths.
4. Cut the roots off the daikon sprouts, and cut the cherry tomatoes into wedges.
5. Parboil the shimeji and dress with the soy sauce.

Make 2 cones of each variety. Place a small amount of sushi rice on a piece of toasted nori, then add half of the ingredients (fig. 2) and roll up in a cone (fig. 3). Repeat, using the second half of the ingredients. Do this for each of the 5 varieties, making 10 cones in all.

JUMBO SUSHI ROLLS
(Makes 1 roll, cut into 8 pieces)

Jumbo sushi rolls are very popular as picnic and lunchbox treats in Japan. Make sure to roll these carefully and tightly so they hold together.

---

2 1/2 cups white sushi rice
2 sheets nori

1 large piece (about 6 by 2³/4 inches) deep-fried tofu (or 2 small pieces)
1 cup soup stock
1 tablespoon mirin
1 tablespoon soy sauce

1 square konnyaku
4 dried shiitake
2 cups soup stock
2 tablespoons mirin
2 tablespoons soy sauce

1/2 medium carrot, cut into sticks 1/2 inch on a side
1/2 handful of spinach or other green leafy vegetable
15 green beans
6 okra
2 asparagus spears

1/4 boiled bamboo shoot
1 cup soup stock
1 tablespoon mirin
1 tablespoon soy sauce

12 inches kampyo
1 cup water
1 tablespoon mirin
1 tablespoon soy sauce

2 pieces freeze-dried tofu
1 1/2 cups soup stock
2 tablespoons mirin
1 teaspoon salt
1/4 teaspoon turmeric
2 inches mountain yam or daikon

2 tablespoons red ginger pickles

Simmer the deep-fried tofu in 1 cup water for 5 minutes. Drain and press out as much oil as possible, then simmer in 1 cup soup stock, 1 tablespoon mirin, and 1 tablespoon soy sauce for 5 minutes. Cut open three sides of the pocket and open the tofu out to a flat sheet as in figure 1.

Simmer the konnyaku and shiitake in 2 cups soup stock, 2 tablespoons mirin, and 2 tablespoons soy sauce for 8 minutes and cut into thin slices 1/2 inch wide.

Parboil the carrot, spinach, green beans, okra, and asparagus in lightly salted water to bring out the flavor and color (you can parboil the vegetables in succession in the same water).

Cut the boiled bamboo shoot into sticks 1/2 inch on a side and simmer for 8 minutes in 1 cup soup stock, 1 tablespoon mirin, and 1 tablespoon soy sauce.

Reconstitute the freeze-dried tofu in warm water, then press it dry. Simmer the tofu in 1 1/2 cups soup stock, 2 tablespoons mirin, 1 teaspoon salt, and 1/4 teaspoon turmeric for 8 minutes, then slice into 1/2 inch strips.

Spread the sheet of deep-fried tofu on a cutting board and place the green beans, mountain yam, and carrots in the center. Roll the tofu up, as in figure 2.

Place the 2 sheets of nori on the rolling mat, as in figure 3. Overlap them about 1/2 inch and join them by smashing a few grains of the sushi rice between them, creating a rice paste. (You can also join the nori sheets with water, but the rice paste is stronger.)

Spread the sushi rice on the joined sheets of nori to a thickness of about 1/2 inch, reserving 3/4 inch of nori on the far edge.

Arrange the asparagus, bamboo shoot, okra, kampyo, spinach, dried tofu, shiitake, konnyaku, and deep-fried tofu roll in horizontal rows on the bed of rice. Leave uncovered about 3 1/4 inches of rice on the far edge and about 2 inches of rice on the near edge, as in figure 4.

Roll up the jumbo roll so that the uncovered rice at both ends overlaps. Cut the roll into 8 pieces and serve cut side up with a garnish of red ginger pickles.

TOSSED
SUSHI

MIYABIZUSHI
(Serves 4)

"Miyabi" means elegant or refined, and this sushi, with its colorful ingredients mixed lightly together, certainly fits the bill. Serving it in a beautiful utensil, as in the photograph, will make it even more appealing.

---

4 cups white sushi rice

$^1/_2$ small lotus root tuber
I teaspoon vinegar
$^1/_4$ cup apple cider vinegar
I tablespoon honey
$^1/_2$ tablespoon salt

4 pieces freeze-dried tofu
$^2/_3$ cup soup stock
$^1/_4$ teaspoon tumeric
I teaspoon mirin
$^1/_2$ teaspoon salt

6 shiitake
I teaspoon mirin
I teaspoon soy sauce

16 inches kampyo
$^1/_4$ teaspoon salt
I cup soup stock
I teaspoon mirin
I teaspoon soy sauce

$^1/_2$ carrot
dash of mirin
10 snow peas
2 tablespoons white sesame seeds

GARNISHES
cherry blossoms pickled in salt, sansho leaves, red ginger pickles

Peel and cut the lotus into thin slices, then simmer for 5 minutes in 2 cups boiling water with a teaspoon of vinegar. Drain.

Marinate the lotus-root slices in 1/4 cup apple cider vinegar, 1 tablespoon honey, and 1/2 tablespoon salt.

Soak the freeze-dried tofu in hot water until soft, then gently squeeze out all excess moisture. Simmer the reconstituted tofu in the soup stock with turmeric, mirin, and salt for 5 minutes, then cut into attractive shapes.

Soak the shiitake in 1 cup water for 1 hour, then drain, but reserve the water. Cut each mushroom into 6 pieces and simmer in the water, with 1 teaspoon mirin and 1 teaspoon soy sauce for 5 minutes.

Rinse the kampyo under cool water and then rub salt into it. Let it sit for 2 minutes, squeeze out any excess liquid, and soak it in water for 5 minutes. Simmer in 1 cup soup stock, 1 teaspoon mirin, and 1 teaspoon soy sauce for 5 minutes. Cut into 1/2-inch lengths.

Slice the carrot thinly and then cut most of the slices into decorative shapes. Dice any remaining slices. Simmer all the carrot slices in lightly salted water with a dash of mirin for 3 minutes.

Parboil the snow peas in lightly salted water for 1 minute and then plunge into cold water for 30 seconds to cool quickly. Cut them diagonally into pieces of equal size.

Roast the white sesame seeds in a pan with no oil and then chop finely.

Set aside a small amount of each of the ingredients to use as a garnish, and toss the rest with the sushi rice. Garnish with the reserved ingredients and cherry blossoms, sansho leaves, and red ginger pickles.

SUSHI SALAD WITH WILD VEGETABLES
(Serves 4)

"Sushi salad" (chirashizushi) contains a variety of ingredients mixed with and also dressed over a bed of sushi rice. This recipe provides a variety of tastes and textures with wild vegetables. Burdock and fern fronds (zemmai) are typical wild vegetables seasonally available in Oriental food stores, but feel free to experiment as long as you provide a variety of tastes, colors, and textures.

---

4 cups sushi rice with millet
¹/₂ small carrot
6 shiitake (reconstituted with 1 cup water)
1 tablespoon soy sauce
1 tablespoon mirin

¹/₂ cup fern fronds (zemmai)
1 tablespoon salt
soup stock (enough to cover ingredients)
1 tablespoon light soy sauce
1 tablespoon mirin

¹/₂ butterburr stem (or ¹/₂ burdock root)
1 cup soup stock
1 tablespoon mirin
1 tablespoon soy sauce

1 cup chopped boiled bamboo shoots

1 cup bean curd lees, or ¹/₂ square of tofu
¹/₂ teaspoon turmeric
2 tablespoons apple vinegar
1 tablespoon honey
1 teaspoon salt

Cut the carrot into thin round slices and then quarter each slice. Parboil in lightly salted water for 3 minutes.

Cut about $1/2$ of the shiitake into $1/3$-inch slices lengthwise and dice the remainder. Simmer all the shiitake in the 1 cup water used to reconstitute it, adding 1 tablespoon soy sauce and 1 tablespoon mirin, for about 8 minutes.

To remove bitterness, rub the zemmai fronds with 1 tablespoon salt and then pour hot water over them and soak until the water is cool. Rinse once more and cut into $1/3$-inch lengths. Simmer in enough soup stock to cover, with soy sauce and mirin, for about 5 minutes.

Parboil the butterburr with salt for 1 minute, then peel and dice. If you are using burdock instead, slice (without peeling) as if sharpening a pencil with a knife and simmer for 8 minutes in 1 cup soup stock, 1 tablespoon mirin, and 1 tablespoon soy sauce.

Place the bean-curd lees or tofu, tumeric, apple vinegar, honey, and salt in a small pan and scramble the mixture over low heat until well broken up and fairly dry.

Stir most of the scrambled bean curd lees into the sushi rice, reserving about $1/5$ to sprinkle on top. Serve in a large dish, and garnish with the remaining ingredients.

MOSAIC SUSHI
(Serves 4)

The variety of colorful ingredients suggested the name of this dish. It's not important to measure the exact quantities of the vegetables that make up this mosaic. Just prepare roughly equal amounts of each, 1 to 1 1/2 cups in total.

---

4 cups white sushi rice
2 tablespoons red bell pepper
2 tablespoons yellow bell pepper
2 tablespoons green bell pepper
2 tablespoons Japanese pumpkin
2 tablespoons shimeji mushrooms
2 tablespoons broccoli
2 tablespoons red onion
2 tablespoons corn
4 lettuce leaves
1 radish

Cut the peppers and pumpkin into 1/2 inch cubes and parboil in lightly salted water.

Break the broccoli and shimeji mushroom into small florets and clumps, parboil in lightly salted water, and cut into 1/2 inch cubes.

Cut the red onion into 1/2 inch cubes and sprinkle lightly with salt.

Combine all these ingredients and the corn with the white sushi rice, folding them in gently. Lay a bed of lettuce leaf in a bowl and arrange the sushi rice on top of it. Slice the radish thinly and use as a garnish.

4-BEAN SUSHI
(Serves 4)

Think of this as a bean salad with sushi rice. Any small red bean can be substituted for red soy beans, and green peas can be substituted for fresh green soy beans.

---

3 cups brown sushi rice

$^1/_4$ cup each of black beans, soy beans, red soy beans, and fresh green soy beans

$^1/_2$ medium carrot
red ginger pickles

Prepare each variety of bean separately by boiling until tender.

Cut the carrot into 2-inch cubes and parboil in lightly salted water.

Add the beans and carrots to the brown sushi rice, stir, and serve with a garnish of red ginger pickles.

SUSHI IN A PUMPKIN CUP
(Makes 1 large cup or 4 small cups)

Japanese pumpkins, or kabocha, are much smaller and more tender than the average Western pumpkin, and their flesh is delicious—clean-tasting and slightly sweet—when steamed. They are available in Asian food stores (many Asian cuisines use similar pumpkins as well), and health food stores. Don't try to substitute a Western pumpkin.

---

2 cups white sushi rice
2 tablespoons ground white sesame seeds

1 Japanese pumpkin, about 8 inches in diameter, or
**   4 smaller ones, about 5 inches in diameter**

small amount of the inner flesh of the pumpkins, cut into matchsticks
1 tablespoon shredded pickled plum
a few sprigs of parsley

Mix 2 tablespoons ground white sesame seeds into the sushi rice.

Cut off the top 1/4 of the pumpkin as a lid, as in the figure. Clean out the remaining 3/4, removing seeds and pulp and rinsing carefully. Scoop out a small amount of the flesh, parboil in lightly salted water, and chop into matchsticks.

Place pumpkin (and lid) in a steamer and steam until tender.

Fill the pumpkin with sushi rice and garnish with the pumpkin matchsticks, the shredded pickled plum, and the parsley.

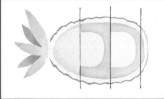

PINEAPPLE FRUIT CUP SUSHI
(Makes 2 cups)

This and the following recipe are nontraditional sushi dishes, but the vinegar in sushi rice complements tart fruits exceptionally well.

---

2 cups white sushi rice

1 fresh pineapple
2 tablespoons pineapple juice
2 tablespoons pineapple flesh
1/4 kiwi
1 loquat or 1/3 cup of mango, papaya, or apricot
5 cherries

Cut a pineapple as shown in the figure and scoop out the flesh to form 2 cups to hold the sushi. Reserve 2 tablespoons juice and 2 tablespoons flesh.

Peel the kiwi and loquat (or substitute) and cut them and the pineapple flesh into bite-size chunks.

Stir the pineapple juice into the sushi rice. Place the sushi rice in the pineapple cups and decorate with the pineapple flesh, kiwi, loquat, and cherries.

GRAPEFRUIT CUP SUSHI
(Makes 2 cups)

---

2 cups white sushi rice

2 grapefruits
1 okra
$^1/_5$ medium carrot
$^1/_2$ Japanese cucumber
$^1/_6$ onion
4 cherry tomatoes
2 tablespoons grapefruit juice
2 leaves lettuce

Cut $^1/_3$ off the top of each grapefruit, as in the figure, and remove the flesh from the remaining $^2/_3$ to form a cup. Cut the flesh of 1 grapefruit into bite-size chunks.

Parboil the okra and slice thinly.

Cut the carrot into $^1/_4$-inch cubes and parboil in lightly salted water.

Cut the cucumber into $^1/_2$-inch cubes and slice the onion thinly.

Slice the cherry tomatoes.

Stir the grapefruit juice into the sushi rice. Place a leaf of lettuce in each grapefruit cup, fill them with the sushi rice, and decorate with the okra, carrot, cucumber, onion, cherry tomatoes, and grapefruit flesh.

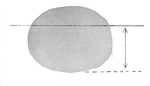

SUSHI SALAD WITH ONIONS
(Serves 4)

The onions add a distinctive bite to this sushi salad. Slicing them paper thin is important, so they don't overpower the rice.

---

4 cups white sushi rice

$^1/_2$ white or yellow onion
$^1/_2$ red onion
$^1/_8$ medium-size Japanese pumpkin
2 small Japanese bell peppers or $^1/_2$ green American bell pepper

4 leaves lettuce
4 cherry tomatoes

Slice the onions in half lengthwise and then slice thinly.
    Slice the pumpkin into matchsticks and parboil in lightly salted water.
    Slice the bell peppers thinly into rings.
    Stir all of these ingredients into the sushi rice. Serve the rice over a bed of lettuce and garnish with the cherry tomatoes cut in half lengthwise.

SUMMER SUSHI
(Serves 4)

With wakame seaweed, cucumber, and white sesame, this sushi has a light, cool taste, especially refreshing on a hot summer day.

---

4 cups brown sushi rice

$^1/_3$ medium carrot
$^1/_2$ medium Japanese cucumber
$^1/_4$ onion

$^1/_3$ cup reconstituted wakame
3 tablespoons white sesame seeds

10 thinly sliced green shiso leaves and red ginger pickles as garnish

---

Cut the carrot into thin slices, then cut the slices into quarters. Slice the cucumber thinly and sprinkle the slices with salt to wrinkle them. Cut the onion into quarters and then slice thinly. Chop the wakame coarsely. Chop the sesame seeds.

Mix all of the ingredients in with the sushi rice and garnish with the chopped shiso leaves. Serve the red ginger pickles on the side.

GOMOKU SUSHI
(Serves 4)

"Gomoku" means "five varieties," and it's frequently used for dishes with a mix of a wide variety of ingredients. In this recipe, there are actually six: carrot, konnyaku, shiitake mushrooms, lotus root, corn, and green beans.

---

3 cups white sushi rice

$1/3$ medium carrot

$1/3$ square konnyaku
I cup soup stock
I tablespoon mirin
I tablespoon soy sauce

4 dried shiitake
I tablespoon mirin
I tablespoon soy sauce

$1/2$ small lotus root tuber
I tablespoon vinegar

$1/4$ cup frozen or canned corn

6 green beans

Cut the carrot into $1/3$-inch cubes and parboil in lightly salted water.

Simmer the konnyaku in lightly salted water for a few minutes, then drain and cut into $1/3$-inch cubes. Simmer the cubes in I cup soup stock, I tablespoon mirin, and I tablespoon soy sauce for 5 to 6 minutes.

Reconstitute the dried shiitake in I cup water for I hour, then cut into $1/3$-inch cubes. Simmer in the water, I tablespoon mirin, and I tablespoon soy sauce for 5 to 6 minutes.

Cut the lotus tuber into $1/2$ inch cubes and simmer in 2 cups water and I tablespoon vinegar for 5 minutes.

Parboil the beans in lightly salted water and cut into 1/3-inch lengths.

Mix all the ingredients in with the sushi rice, toss, and serve.

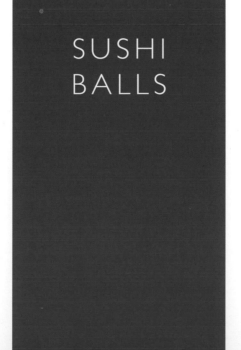

SUSHI
BALLS

CHERRY SUSHI
(Makes 8 pieces)

Cherry blossoms are one of the most beloved flowers in Japan, a symbol of spring and evanescent beauty. Cherry tree leaves, usually pickled, are used as a wrapping for traditional Japanese sweets. They have a faint but pleasant fragrance and taste. This recipe calls for fresh cherry tree leaves, which you should wash and dry carefully before using. You can also use the pickled leaves, available in Asian food stores, but rinse off as much salt as possible. Pickled cherry blossoms are also available in Asian food stores.

---

2 cups white sushi rice

8 pickled cherry blossoms
8 fresh cherry tree leaves

Rinse the pickled cherry blossoms to remove excess salt and mince finely. Mix well into the sushi rice. Wash the cherry tree teaves and pat dry. Form the sushi rice into balls and wrap them in the cherry leaves. Serve.

SASA SUSHI

The leaves of the variety of bamboo called sasa in Japanese are often used to wrap sushi, and lend it a distinctive, fresh aroma, though they are not eaten. Sasa can sometimes be purchased in Oriental food shops. You can also substitute any attractive edible salad leaf—lettuce, cabbage, or red or green Belgian endive, for example—with the bonus that you can eat the wrapping.

---

2 cups white sushi rice

$^1/_3$ **cup Japanese pumpkin, cut into $^1/_2$-inch cubes**
5 fresh green peas
I medium onion
$^3/_4$ **inches carrot**
2 tablespoons red soy beans, azuki beans, or other small red beans
2 tablespoons fresh green soy beans or green peas

red ginger pickles as garnish

Cut the pumpkin into $^1/_3$-inch cubes and parboil in lightly salted water.
    Parboil the peas as well.
    Peel the onion and cut it into large wedges. Break the wedges apart layer by layer and parboil in lightly salted water.
    Cut the carrot into $^1/_3$-inch cubes and parboil in lightly salted water.
    Boil the red beans and the green soy beans in salted water until tender.
    Divide the sushi rice in half and mix the pumpkin and fresh peas into one half and the red and green soybeans into the other. Place a small amount of the pumpkin-pea sushi in the center of a sasa leaf and wrap the ends around as in the photo.
    Shape the bean sushi into little boats and serve on the onion wedges. Garnish with red ginger pickles.

MUSHROOM SUSHI
(Makes 4 pieces)

These sushi balls, topped with the large caps of fresh shiitake mus-
rooms, are a delicious and nonfattening alternative to stuffed mushrooms as an hors d'oeuvre.

---

2 cups white sushi rice
2 tablespoons white sesame seeds

4 large fresh shiitake (just the caps)
3 tablespoons mirin
2 tablespoons soy sauce
I tablespoon sake

poppy seeds and red ginger pickles as garnish

Toast the white sesame seeds lightly in a nonstick pan with no oil.
Crush them in a mortar and mix them with the sushi rice.

Mix the mirin, soy sauce, and sake and simmer the fresh shiitake
mushroom caps in the liquid for a minute or two. Remove the caps and
drain well.

Form a ball of sushi rice, place a mushroom cap on top of it, and
sprinkle with poppy seeds. Serve with red ginger pickles as garnish.

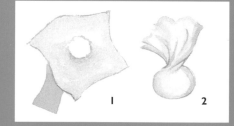

CAMELLIA SUSHI
(Makes 12 pieces)

In this recipe, the sushi balls are shaped into the deep, cuplike form of camellia flowers, which are often red-and-white splashed. The garnish in the center recalls the camellia's conspicuous stamens, and the camellia-leaf garnish adds to the effect, though they are not edible.

---

2 cups white sushi rice

$1/3$ medium carrot
$1/2$ cup pink sushi rice
$1/2$ cup white sushi rice

DECORATION
a few fresh green soybeans or green peas
small amount of shredded pickled plum
red ginger pickles as garnish
camellia leaves

Mince the carrot and parboil in lightly salted water. Mix into 2 cups white sushi rice.

Divide the rice mixture into 4 equal portions. Place one portion of the rice in a wet tea towel and twist firmly, so as to leave an impression of the folds of the towel. These should resemble the divisions between the petals of a camellia blossom, as in the photograph. Do the same for the remaining seven portions.

Parboil the fresh green soybeans or green peas in lightly salted water for 5 minutes, then press them or or a small dab of shredded pickled plum in the center of each "blossom."

Mix the $1/2$ cup pink sushi rice and $1/2$ cup white sushi rice together. Divide into 4 equal portions. Prepare and decorate as above. Serve on a bed of camellia leaves.

SUSHI CREPES
(Makes ten crepes, two of each variety)

This is certainly an innovative way to present sushi, and the pink, white, yellow, and brown rice makes for a very colorful dish.

---

1 1/2 cups fine rice flour
1 1/2 cups water
1 teaspoon salt
1 teaspoon sesame oil

1/2 cup white sushi rice
1 teaspoon seaweed flakes
2 pickled cherry blossoms, finely chopped

1/2 cup pink sushi rice
1/5 okra, sliced thinly

1/2 cup pink sushi rice
1/2 teaspoon white sesame seeds
2 boiled black beans

1/2 cup brown sushi rice
1/2 teaspoon black sesame seed
a small amount of carrot, diced and parboiled

1/2 cup yellow sushi rice
2 boiled fresh green soybeans or green peas
1/2 teaspoon shredded pickled plum

1 radish, 1 cherry tomato, 1/2 Japanese cucumber as garnish

Prepare each of the five sushi "fillings" above and put aside.

Mix the rice flour, water, and salt together in a bowl. Heat a frying pan and pour the sesame oil into it. Pour a small amount of the batter into the pan and swirl the pan to create a crepe about 4 inches in diameter. The batter should make about ten crepes.

Form the crepes into cups and fill the cups with the 5 different sushi rice mixtures and their garnishes. Serve the crepe cups on a plate and decorate the serving plate with the radish, cherry tomatoes, and sliced Japanese cucumber.

SUSHI BALLS
(Makes 12 pieces, 4 of each variety)

This recipe uses carrot, pumpkin, and radish as the outer layer for three kinds of sushi balls, with sushi rice in the center. Each variety of sushi ball has its own garnish, too.

---

2 cups white sushi rice

1 medium carrot
4 black beans
4 fresh green soy beans or green peas
4 red soy beans

1 cup Japanese pumpkin, cut into matchsticks
4 stems daikon sprouts
$^1/_2$ inch carrot
4 sprigs pineapple sage

5 radishes
small amounts of broccoli florets, canned or frozen corn, and shredded pickled plum

---

Cut the carrot into thin matchsticks and parboil in lightly salted water. Cook each of the three varieties of beans.

Cut the pumpkin into thin matchsticks and parboil in lightly salted water. Cut off the stems of the daikon sprouts; retain only the leaves. Cut the carrot into $^1/_2$ inch cubes and parboil in lightly salted water.

Slice the radishes thinly. Parboil the broccoli florets in lightly salted water. Slice the remaining carrot and pumpkin into thin matchsticks.

Wet a clean tea towel or pastry cloth and wring it dry. To make the carrot balls, place a small amount of the parboiled carrot matchsticks in the center of the towel and place it in the palm of your hand (fig. 1). Place a larger amount of sushi rice on top of the carrot, and then form it into a ball using the tea towel. Twist the towel to compact the ball (fig. 2), making a small indentation in the top, as in the photograph.

Make the pumpkin and radish balls in the same way.

Garnish the carrot balls with the red, green, and black beans; the pumpkin balls with the daikon sprout leaves, carrot cubes, and pineapple sage; and the radish balls with the broccoli florets, corn, and shredded pickled plum.

SUSHI POCKETS AND PRESSED SUSHI

INARIZUSHI POCKETS
(Makes 20 pockets)

Inarizushi is named after the rice god, who is often pictured as a fox and is said to be very fond of deep-fried tofu. Because Inarizushi are so handy, they make a perfect snack or picnic treat.

---

4 cups white sushi rice

small amounts of the following (use to taste):
carrot
shiitake (reconstituted in water)
soy sauce
mirin (mix into sushi rice)
pine nuts
sesame seeds

10 sheets deep-fried tofu
2 cups soup stock
2 tablespoons soy sauce
2 tablespoons mirin

20 mitsuba
20 pickled cherry blossoms

Coarsely chop the carrot and shiitake. Place in a pan and barely cover with water, add a dash of soy sauce and mirin, and simmer until the liq-uid evaporates. Mix them into the sushi rice with the pine nuts and sesame seeds.

Simmer the deep-fried tofu sheets in a pan of water for 4 to 5 min-utes. Allow the water to cool, then gently squeeze any excess water out of the tofu with your hands. Place the tofu back into the pan, then add the 2 cups soup stock, 2 tablespoons of soy sauce, and 2 tablespoons of mirin. Simmer until most of the stock is absorbed by the tofu.

Drain and pat the deep-fried tofu dry. Cut each sheet in half and open the cut edge to form tofu pockets. To provide visual variety, you can turn half of the pockets inside out. Stuff sushi rice into the pockets, tie them closed with the mitsuba stems, and garnish with the pickled cherry blossoms.

Lotus root, burdock, snow peas, and hijiki can also be mixed into the sushi rice to create variations.

THREE-COLOR SUSHI POCKETS
(Makes 8 pockets)

---

4 cups brown sushi rice
2 tablespoons finely chopped sesame seeds

4 sheets deep-fried tofu
soup stock, enough to cover tofu
I tablespoon soy sauce
I tablespoon mirin

$^1/_2$ small carrot
10 snow peas
8 shiitake
I cup water
2 tablespoons soy sauce
2 tablespoons mirin

pickled cherry blossoms as garnish

Mix the sesame seeds in with the rice.

Simmer the deep-fried tofu sheets in a pan of water for 4 to 5 minutes. Drain and discard the water. Allow the tofu to cool, then gently squeeze out any excess water with your hands. Place the tofu back into the pan, then add the soup stock, I tablespoon soy sauce, and I tablespoon mirin. Simmer until most of the stock is absorbed by the tofu.

Cut the carrot into matchsticks and parboil in lightly salted water for I minute.

Parboil the snow peas in lightly salted water for I minute, then plunge them into cold water to cool. Cut on the diagonal and sprinkle lightly with salt.

Reconstitute the shiitake by soaking them in I cup water for about I hour. Drain, but save the water. Cut the shiitake lengthwise into strips. Return the strips to the soaking water and simmer for 5 minutes with 2 tablespoons soy sauce and 2 tablespoons mirin.

Cut each sheet of deep-fried tofu in half and open the cut end to make a pocket. Stuff the sushi rice into the tofu pockets and heap the carrot, snow peas, and shiitake on top.

Rinse the pickled cherry blossoms quickly in hot water to remove excess salt and use as a garnish.

SUSHI FIGS
(Makes 16 figs)

There's no fig in this recipe, but if you are careful the finished product will resemble a ripe fig.

---

2 cups white sushi rice
1 cup pink sushi rice
4 sheets nori

$^1/_2$ cup tofu lees or $^1/_2$ block fresh tofu
1 pinch turmeric
1 teaspoon salt
1 tablespoon vinegar
1 teaspoon honey

Place the tofu lees, turmeric, salt, vinegar, and honey in a frying pan and saute until scrambled into dry, loose pieces. If using fresh tofu, simmer it in water for 5 minutes, then drain and press out as much liquid as possible. Saute with the other ingredients, stirring until most of the water has evaporated and the mixture is scrambled and somewhat dry.

Cut each sheet of nori into 4 (fig. 1). With a pair of scissors, cut an X (as shown in the illustration) about 1$^1/_4$ in length in the middle of each square (fig. 2).

Form a small ball of white sushi rice about 1$^1/_4$ inches in diameter. Place a dab of pink sushi rice on top of it, then another dab of the fried mixture. Cover this with the square of nori, the X on top (fig. 3), and gently wrap the nori around the rice ball, causing the X to open as in the photograph (fig. 4).

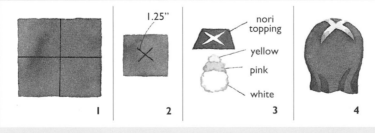

	1.25"	nori topping	
		yellow	
		pink	
		white	
1	**2**	**3**	**4**

SUSHI AND TOFU SANDWICH
(Makes 8 pieces)

The freeze-dried tofu in this recipe is split and stuffed to resemble a sandwich. The freeze-drying process makes this tofu strong enough to hold together in a way that fresh tofu would not, and the turmeric gives it an attractive bright yellow coloring.

---

2 cups white sushi rice
3 tablespoons white sesame seeds

¹/₄ medium carrot

4 pieces freeze-dried tofu (koyadofu)
2 cups soup stock
¹/₃ teaspoon turmeric
2 tablespoons mirin
I teaspoon salt

4 dried shiitake
I cup water
I tablespoon soy sauce
I tablespoon mirin
¹/₂ teaspoon white sesame seeds

Mix the 3 tablespoons white sesame seeds with the white sushi rice.

Mince the carrot and parboil it in lightly salted water.

Reconstitute the freeze-dried tofu in warm water, then press it dry. Simmer the tofu in the soup stock, turmeric, mirin, and salt for 10 minutes. Drain and cut in half diagonally (fig. 1). With a sharp knife, slice the diagonal edge open to make a pocket (fig. 2).

Mix the minced carrot into the sushi rice and stuff the mixture into the tofu pockets.

Reconstitute the dried shiitake in 1 cup of water, then simmer for about 6 minutes in the water, soy sauce, and mirin. Slice into thin strips and sprinkle with the white sesame seeds.

Serve the sushi with the shiitake on the side.

SUSHI DIAMONDS
(Makes 9 pieces)

This is a kind of pressed sushi, or oshizushi. In Japan, pressed sushi is made in a wooden box with a fitted lid that can be pressed down over the sushi rice to pack it down firmly, and a removable bottom. A rectangular pan with straight sides can be substituted. If you don't have a fitted lid, cut a piece of heavy cardboard and wrap it in plastic wrap. Japanese food stores sell sushi presses. They are usually rectangular, but also come in decorative shapes. A square mold 7 inches on a side will result in 9 sushi diamonds.

6 cups white sushi rice

2 tablespoons seaweed powder
2–3 tablespoons red plum vinegar
1 teaspoon turmeric

1 small carrot
10 shiitake, reconstituted
small amounts of soup stock, salt, mirin, and soy sauce

red ginger pickles, pickled cherry blossoms, parsley or pineapple sage
    as garnish

Divide the sushi rice into 3 equal portions. Mix the seaweed powder into one, to create green sushi rice. Mix the red plum vinegar into the second portion, creating pink sushi rice, and mix the turmeric into the third, creating yellow sushi rice.

Slice the carrot into thin matchsticks and simmer in just enough soup stock to cover, with a dash of salt and mirin.

Slice the shiitake into thick matchsticks and simmer in just enough soup stock to cover, with soy sauce and mirin.

Press the green sushi rice into a rectangular pan or mold with square sides. Spread a layer of carrots, then press in the red sushi rice. Spread a layer of shiitake and then press in the yellow sushi rice. Press and compact the sushi with a lid or another tool.

Remove the sushi from the mold and cut it into diamonds. Garnish with red pickled ginger (in the photograph, the ginger is cut into butterfly shapes using a vegetable cutter), pickled cherry blossoms, and parsley.

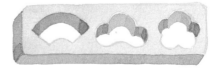

MINIATURE PRESSED SUSHI
(Makes 12 pieces, 4 of each kind)

Make this recipe only if you can find interesting molds—cookie molds will do, but they must be deep enough to hold three layers.

---

1 1/2 cups white sushi rice
1 tablespoon white sesame seeds
1 1/2 cups pink sushi rice
1 1/2 cups yellow sushi rice

1/3 medium burdock root
2 teaspoons soy sauce
1 teaspoon mirin
1 cup water

1/3 medium carrot
1/2 teaspoon salt
2/3 cup water

1/3 Japanese cucumber
1 teaspoon shredded pickled plum
1 teaspoon white miso
3 radishes
a few pieces of carrot cut in a star pattern and sliced thinly
1 okra, sliced thinly
5 cherries

Mix the sesame seeds into the white sushi rice.

Slice the burdock into matchsticks and simmer in the soy sauce, mirin, and water over low heat for 10 minutes.

Slice the carrots into matchsticks and simmer in the salt and water for 3 minutes.

Rinse the molds. Press a layer of white sushi rice into a mold. Top this with a layer of either carrot or burdock, and then press in another layer of white sushi rice.

Proceed in the same way with the pink and yellow sushi rice: rice—vegetable—rice. Make 4 pieces of pressed sushi from each color of rice.

Decorate the top of each piece with either cucumber slices and shredded pickled plum or radish slices and carrot stars and a touch of white miso. Serve on a plate sprinkled with the okra slices, carrot stars, and cherries.

SUSHI RICE CAKE
(Makes 8 slices)

---

1 1/2 cups white sushi rice
seaweed flakes

1 1/2 cups pink sushi rice
1 1/2 cups yellow sushi rice

1 block fresh tofu
3 tablespoons white miso
1 teaspoon salt
1 tablespoon sesame cream
1 tablespoon apple cider vinegar

1/3 medium lotus root
1/3 Japanese cucumber
4 cherry tomatoes
1/3 carrot cut in a star pattern
8 garlic chive sprouts or 4 asparagus spears

1/3 cup shimeji
1 tablespoon sake
1/2 teaspoon salt
2 tablespoons water

2 tablespoons raisins
6 cherries
8 leaves lettuce

Prepare "tofu cheese" by simmering the tofu in water for about 5 minutes, then pressing it through a strainer. Add the white miso, salt, sesame cream, and apple cider vinegar and stir until smooth.

Peel the lotus root and slice into thin matchsticks. Parboil in water with a dash of vinegar.

Cut the cucumber in half lengthwise, then slice thinly on a diagonal.

Slice the cherry tomatoes into rounds.

Use a vegetable cutter to cut the carrot into thin, star-shaped slices, and then parboil together with the garlic chive sprouts (or asparagus spears) in lightly salted water.

Simmer the shimeji in the sake, salt, and water mixture in a covered pan over very low heat until the liquid is absorbed.

Spread plastic wrap in a circular mold and press in the white sushi rice, followed by the pink and the yellow, in three distinct layers. Remove it from the mold and decorate with the tofu cheese and vegetables, as shown in the illustration.

Cut into slices and serve on a plate with the lettuce leaves, cherries, and raisins.

The "weathermark" identifies this book as a production of Weatherhill, Inc., publishers of fine books on Asia and the Pacific. Editorial supervision: Jeffrey Hunter. Book and cover design: Mariana Canelo. Production supervision: Bill Rose. Printed and bound by Oceanic Graphic Printing, China. The typeface used is Gill Sans.